YLP YOUNG LEARNER'S

GW00598898

LOOK-n-LEARN

EARTH

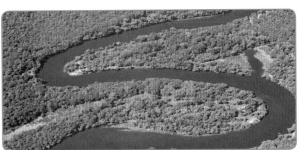

Earth

We live on the planet Earth. It is the only known planet in the solar system that supports life. About 70% of the Earth's surface is covered with water.

Moon

The Moon is the only natural satellite which revolves around the Earth. It does not have light of its own. It reflects the light of the Sun.

Crust

The crust is the outermost layer of the Earth. It is composed of elements like silicon, aluminium, iron, etc.

Mantle

The mantle is the second layer of the Earth. This layer is about 2900 km thick.

Core

The core is the innermost layer of the Earth. It is separated into the liquid outer core and the solid inner core.

Atmosphere

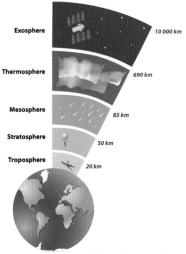

Atmosphere is the blanket of air surrounding the Earth. It shields us from the harmful ultraviolet radiation of the Sun. It is made of five layers.

Atmospheric pressure

Atmospheric pressure is the force exerted on per unit area of the Earth by the air's weight above that surface. It is measured by a barometer.

Ozone

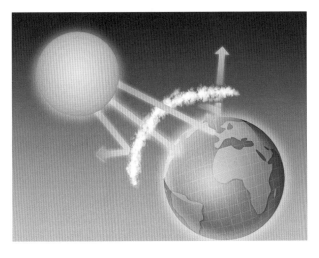

Ozone is a form of oxygen. It forms a layer in the stratosphere. The ozone layer protects the Earth from ultraviolet radiations of the Sun.

Ice age

Ice age refers to the period in history when the Earth was covered in ice. Woolly mammoths lived during this time.

Fossil

A fossil is the remains of a once alive organism from the remote past that got buried deep under the Earth and turned into rock.

Rock

A rock is a naturally occurring solid which is made of one or more minerals. The main categories of rocks are igneous, sedimentary and metamorphic.

Minerals

Minerals are solid materials that form on the Earth naturally. The Earth is made up of several different minerals. All minerals are inorganic.

Continent

A continent is a continuous expanse of land. Africa, Asia, Europe, North America, South America, Australia and Antarctica are continents.

Tectonic plate

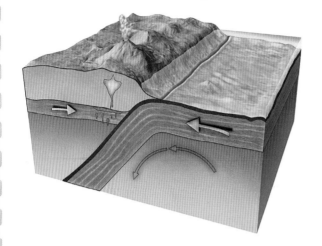

The Earth is made up of big slabs of land called tectonic plates. They vary in size and thickness, and are constantly moving.

Rotation

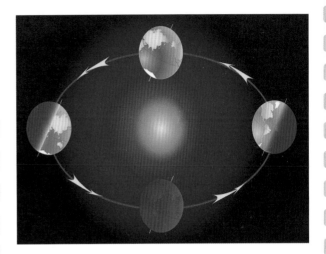

The Earth rotates on its own axis and it takes 24 hours to complete a rotation. This rotation causes days and nights on Earth.

Revolution

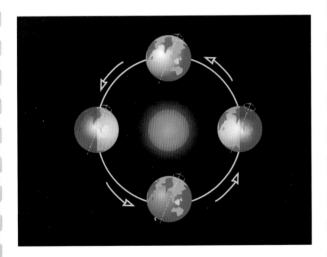

The Earth moves around the Sun in an oval orbit. It takes 365 days to complete one revolution. It orbits the Sun at a speed of 108,000 km/h.

Seasons

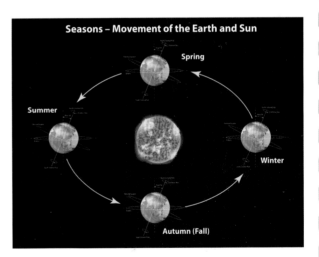

Seasons – Movement of the Earth and Sun

Seasons are the four divisions of the year — summer, winter, spring and autumn — caused due to the varying amount of sunlight that falls on Earth.

Solar eclipse

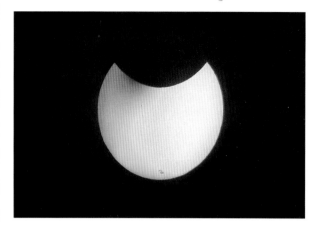

A solar eclipse occurs when the Moon blocks the Sun's rays from falling on the Earth. The Moon casts its shadow on the Earth. The eclipse may be partial or total.

Lunar eclipse

A lunar eclipse occurs when the Earth is between the Moon and the Sun, and the Sun's rays do not fall on the Moon. It occurs about twice in an year and may last for a few hours.

Weather

Weather refers to the climatic conditions of a place at a particular time. Various factors such as humidity, precipitation, wind, etc., affect the weather.

Climate

Climate is a measure of weather conditions such as humidity, wind, temperature, etc. in an area over a long period of time.

Soil

The uppermost layer of the Earth's surface is called soil. It is made of tiny rocks, organic matter, air and water. It serves as the natural medium for the growth of plants.

Plants

Plants are a big group of living things on Earth. Green plants prepare their own food with the help of sunlight, water and carbon dioxide through a process called photosynthesis.

Animals

There is a wide variety of animals on the Earth. They vary in shape, size, habitats, habits, etc. The blue whale is the largest animal on Earth.

Microorganisms

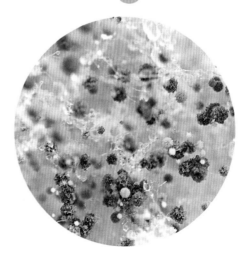

Microorganisms are microscopic organisms such as bacteria, virus, etc. They are too tiny and can be seen only under a microscope.

Plain

Plains are large areas of flat land. They are usually located at the bottom of valleys. They are generally fertile and good for farming.

Plateau

A plateau is a large area of land that is higher than the surrounding land and has a flat top. It is also known as a tableland.

Hill

A hill is an area of land that is higher than the land around it. It is much lower and less steeper than a mountain. It often has a distinct summit.

Mountain

A mountain is a landform which extends above the surrounding land in a limited area. Mount Everest is the highest mountain in the world.

Desert

A desert is an area with little or no rain. It has scarce vegetation. It is generally hot during the day and cold at night. Sahara is the largest desert.

Oasis

An oasis is a small fertile area with water in desert regions. Some plants and trees grow here. Al Ahsa in Saudi Arabia is the largest oasis in the world.

Erosion

Erosion is the process by which the upper layer of soil and rocks are removed by the constant action of wind, water and ice.

Tropical rainforests

Tropical rainforests are areas that receive a lot of rain. The weather in these forests is very humid and warm. Millions of plants and animals live here.

Temperate rainforests

Temperate rainforests receive rain throughout the year. These areas experience mild temperature. They cover a large part of the Earth.

Marine biome

The oceans on the Earth cover 70 percent of its surface. The marine biome includes these oceans, estuaries and coral reefs.

Coral reefs

Coral reefs are ocean habitats rich in life. They are formed when polyps die and leave behind hard, stony structures made of limestone.

Savannah

Savannah is a vast expanse of grassland. The trees are not close to each other, which allows the sunlight to reach the ground.

Tundra

Tundra is an extremely cold and treeless area. It gets scanty rainfall. The two types of tundras are Arctic tundra and Alpine tundra.

Lake

A lake is a small body of water. It is generally surrounded by land. Sometimes, large lakes are also called 'inland seas'.

River

A river is a water body that originates at one source and flows into the sea or the ocean. River water is not salty. The Nile is the largest river in the world.

Sea

Sea is the large expanse of salt water that covers 70 percent of the Earth's surface. Sea water contains salts of chlorine, sodium, sulphur, etc.

Ocean

An ocean is a very large saline water body. There are five oceans on the Earth – Atlantic, Arctic, Indian, Pacific and Southern (Antarctic) ocean.

Tides

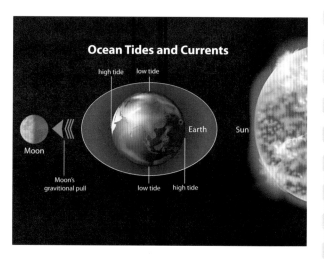

Ocean Tides and Currents

high tide   low tide

Moon

Moon's gravitional pull

low tide   high tide

Earth   Sun

An ocean tide refers to the periodic rise and fall of ocean level. Tides rise and fall twice in about every 24 hours.

Waves

Waves are formed when wind blows across the water surface. Wind pushes the water upwards, but earth's gravity pulls it down, forming waves.

Glacier

A glacier is a huge chunk of ice and snow that moves very slowly from higher to lower ground. This ice is made of fresh water.

Meander

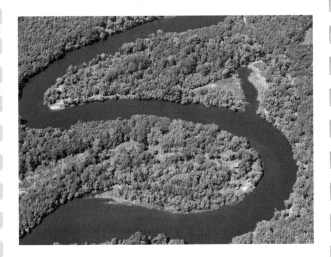

A meander is a bend or curve in the course of a river. The shape of the meander is constantly changed by the flowing river.

Waterfall

A waterfall is formed when water falls off a great height. Victoria Falls is the largest waterfall in the world. It is situated between Zambia and Zimbabwe.

Volcano

A volcano is an opening in the Earth's crust through which molten rocks, gases and steam come out with force. The oldest volcano is Mount Etna, Italy.

Earthquake

The sudden, violent shaking of the Earth's surface is called an earthquake. The strength of the earthquake is measured on the Richter scale.

Forest fire

A forest fire is a natural calamity where fire starts in the forest and spreads wildly, burning down trees. It is also called wildfire.

Tsunami

A tsunami is a huge ocean wave caused due to undersea volcanoes or earthquakes. It causes extensive damage to life and property.

Tornado

A tornado is a violent wind in the shape of a funnel. It rotates and travels long distances, wrecking life and property.

Hurricane

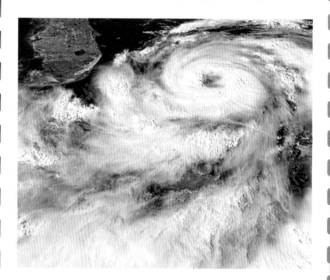

Hurricanes are like tornadoes, but they occur on seas. They form over the sea surface and rotate very fast.

Global warming

Global warming refers to an increase in the average temperature on the Earth due to increased levels of carbon dioxide, CFCs and other pollutants.

Renewable energy

Renewable energy refers to the sources of energy on Earth, namely, Sun, wind, rain, tides, waves, etc., that can be used over and over again.

Geothermal energy

Geothermal energy is derived from the core of the Earth. It is transferred to the surface by geysers and volcanoes.

Hydropower

Hydropower is produced by moving water in dams. Water is dropped on turbines that generate electricity.

Solar power

Solar power is the energy obtained from the Sun. Solar appliances convert heat energy into electric energy.

Wind energy

Windmills, wind pumps and wind turbines are used to convert the power of wind into wind energy.

Tidal energy

The gravitational pull of the moon and the Sun, and the Earth's rotation result in ocean tides, which produce tidal energy.

Wave energy

When powerful winds meet the surface of the water, the friction generated produces wave energy.